love you

very much.

Love,

Scott, Kris
& Kevin

D0040952

Sweet Wishes

You Put a Smile in My Heart

HOLLY POND HILL

BY SUSAN WHEELER

HARVEST HOUSE PUBLISHERS
EUGENE, OREGON 97402

You Put a Smile in My Heart

Text Copyright © 2001 by Harvest House Publishers
Eugene, Oregon 97402

ISBN 0-7369-0514-6

Design and production by
Garborg Design Works, Minneapolis, Minnesota

Scripture quotations are taken from the Holy Bible, New International
Version®, Copyright © 1973, 1978, 1984 by the International Bible
Society. Used by permission of Zondervan Publishing House.

Harvest House Publishers has made every effort to trace the owner-
ship of all poems and quotes. In the event of a question arising from the
use of a poem or quote, we regret any error made and will be pleased
to make the necessary correction in future editions of this book.

Printed in Hong Kong

01 02 03 04 05 06 07 08 09 10 / NG / 10 9 8 7 6 5 4 3 2 1

Blessed are they who have the gift of making friends, for it is one of God's greatest gifts.

AUTHOR UNKNOWN

Soul friendships are
the safety net of the heart.

SUSAN JEFFERS

Laughter is the brush that sweeps
away the cobwebs of the heart.

MORT WALKER

A smile is the
light in your
window that tells
others that there is
a caring, sharing
person inside.

DENIS WAITLEY

We cannot tell the
precise moment when
friendship is formed. As
in filling a vessel drop by
drop there is at last a drop
which makes it run over;
so in a series of kindnesses
there is at last one which
makes the heart run over.

JAMES BOSWELL

Celebrate the happiness that friends are
always giving, make every day a holiday
and celebrate just living!

AMANDA BRADLEY

*Thinking a smile all the time
will keep your face youthful.*

GELETT BURGESS

And the waterlogged Toad came
up slowly but surely over the edge
of the hole, till at last he stood safe
and sound in the hall, streaked
with mud and weed to be sure, and
with the water streaming off him,
but happy and high-spirited as of
old, now that he found himself
once more in the house of a friend.

KENNETH GRAHAME
THE WIND IN THE WILLOWS

Those who bring sunshine into the lives of
others cannot help but keep it for themselves.

SIR JAMES BARRIE

To those in darkest night,

Go be a kindly friend;

Pour love and sunshine on their cares—

And broken lives you'll mend.

ZIMMERMAN

Nothing opens the heart like a true friend,
to whom you may impart griefs, joys, fears,
hopes...and whatever lies upon the heart.

FRANCIS BACON

I had rather have a robin for a friend than a swallow;
for a swallow abides with us only in the summer time,
but a robin cometh to us in the winter.

CHARLES SPURGEON

A friend loves at all times.

THE BOOK OF PROVERBS

Too often we underestimate the power of a touch, a smile, a kind word, a listening ear, an honest compliment, or the smallest act of caring, all of which have the potential to turn a life around.

LEO BUSCAGLIA

Just thinking about a friend makes us want to do a happy dance, because a friend is someone who loves you in spite of your faults.

CHARLES SCHULZ

The road to a friend's
house is never long.

Isaiah 26:8
Susan Wheeler

There is nothing
better than the
encouragement
of a good friend.

KATHERINE BUTLER
HATHAWAY

Few delights can equal the mere presence of one whom we utterly trust.

GEORGE MacDONALD

You gave on the way a pleasant smile,
  And thought no more about it.
It cheered a life that had been dark the while,
  Which might have wrecked without it.
And so for that smile and fruitage rare,
You'll reap a crown sometime—somewhere.

AUTHOR UNKNOWN

The only way to
have a friend is
to be one.

Susan Wheeler

Some friendships are as comforting and
comfortable as a well-worn pair of shoes.
Others are full of excitement and adventure.
The best ones are laced with laughter and
softened with tears and strengthened
with a spiritual bond.

EMILIE BARNES AND DONNA OTTO
FRIENDS OF THE HEART

Love the people with whom
fate brings you together, but
do so with all your heart.

MARCUS AURELIUS

Friendship is warmth in cold, firm ground in a bog.

MILES FRANKLIN

Blessed is the influence of one true, loving soul on another.

GEORGE ELIOT

Life is a chronicle of friendship. Friends create the world anew each day. Without their loving care, courage would not suffice to keep hearts strong for life.

HELEN KELLER

Treasuring your friendship

What brings
joy to the heart
is not so much
the friend's
gift as the
friend's love.

ALFRED OF RIEVAULX

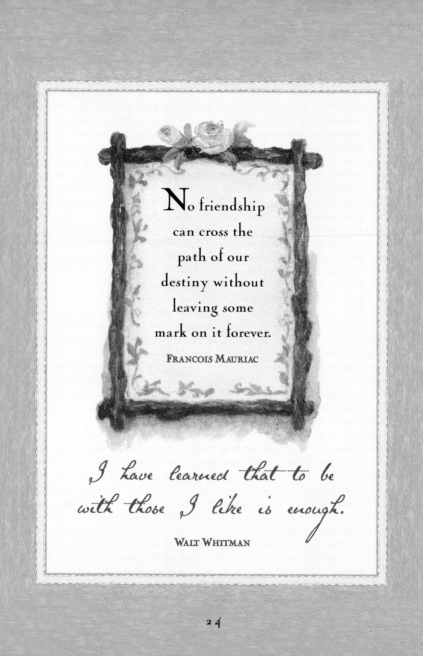

No friendship
can cross the
path of our
destiny without
leaving some
mark on it forever.

FRANCOIS MAURIAC

I have learned that to be
with those I like is enough.

WALT WHITMAN

24

Sometimes just a smile on our face can help to make this world a better place.

ROBERT ALAN

All you need in the world is love and laughter. That's all anybody needs. To have love in one hand and laughter in the other.

AUGUST WILSON

A smile is a curve that sets everything straight.

PHYLLIS DILLER

The glory of friendship is not in the outstretched hand, nor the kindly smile, nor the joy of companionship; it is in the spiritual inspiration that comes to one when he discovers that someone else believes in him and is willing to trust him.

RALPH WALDO EMERSON

The language of friendship is not words but meanings.

HENRY DAVID THOREAU

TO THE ANCIENTS, FRIENDSHIP SEEMED THE HAPPIEST AND MOST FULLY HUMAN OF LOVES; THE CROWN OF LIFE AND THE SCHOOL OF VIRTUE.

C.S. LEWIS

Oh, I have roamed
o'er many lands,
And many friends
I've met;
Not one fair scene
or kindly smile
Can this fond heart forget.

THOMAS HAYNES BAYLY

With a smile that glow'd
Celestial rosy red, love's proper hue.

JOHN MILTON

Smile at each other,

smile at your wife,

smile at your husband,

smile at your children,

smile at each other—

it doesn't matter who it is—

and that will help you to grow up

in greater love for each other.

MOTHER TERESA

Some people come into our lives and quickly go.
Some stay for a while and leave footprints on our hearts.
And we are never, ever the same.

ANONYMOUS

*O*ne should take good care not to grow too wise for so great a pleasure of life as laughter.

JOSEPH ADDISON

*F*riendship is the source of the greatest pleasures, and without friends even the most agreeable pursuits become tedious.

ST. THOMAS AQUINAS

Friendship is the golden thread that ties the heart of all the world.

JOHN EVELYN

The friend in my adversity
I shall always cherish most.
I can better trust those who
helped to relieve the gloom
of my dark hours than those
who are so ready to enjoy
with me the sunshine of
my prosperity.

ULYSSES S. GRANT

It takes a long time to grow an old friend.

JOHN LEONARD

A mirror reflects a man's face,
but what he is really like is shown
by the kind of friends he chooses.

THE BOOK OF PROVERBS

Friends are people you can be quiet with.

AUTHOR UNKNOWN

You cannot hold back a good laugh
any more than you can the tide.
Both are forces of nature.

WILLIAM ROTSLER

My best friend is the one who
brings out the best in me.

HENRY FORD

The man who treasures his friends
is usually solid gold himself.

MARJORIE HOLMES

If a man does not make new acquaintances as he advances through life, he will soon find himself left alone. A man, Sir, should keep his friendship in constant repair.

SAMUEL JOHNSON

Let there be more joy and laughter in your living.

EILEEN CADDY

The person who can bring the spirit of laughter into a room is indeed blessed.

BENNETT CERF

Susan
Wheeler

Acts 4:12

Friendship is one of the sweetest joys of life.

CHARLES SPURGEON

Welcome
Friends

Attention to detail is the secret of success in every sphere of life. Little kindnesses, little acts of consideration, little appreciations, and little confidences are all that most of us are called on to perform, but they are all that are needed to keep a friendship sweet.

HUGH BLACK
FRIENDSHIP

Yes, we must ever be friends; and of all who offer you friendship let me be ever the first, the truest, the nearest and dearest!

HENRY WADSWORTH LONGFELLOW

Laugh and be well.

HORACE GREELY

Friends warm the
world with happiness.

AUTHOR UNKNOWN

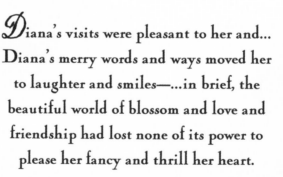

$\mathcal{D}$iana's visits were pleasant to her and...
Diana's merry words and ways moved her
to laughter and smiles—...in brief, the
beautiful world of blossom and love and
friendship had lost none of its power to
please her fancy and thrill her heart.

L. M. MONTGOMERY
ANNE OF GREEN GABLES

The most I can do for my friend is simply be his friend.

HENRY DAVID THOREAU

To laugh with others is one of life's great pleasures.

FRANK TYGER

The shortest distance between new friends is a smile.

AUTHOR UNKNOWN

*A true friend is
the greatest of
all blessings, and
the one that we
take the least care
of all to acquire.*

FRANÇOIS DUC DE LA ROCHEFOUCAULD

Laughter is the most healthful exertion.

CHRISTOPH WILHELM HUFELAND

To make people laugh is a blessing. To have them come back for more is a gift.

ROGER SCOTT